GOD KNOWS IT'S MY BIRTHDAY

by Angela M. Burrin

Illustrated by Andrew Everitt-Stewart

There is someone who knows everything about you. He knows how many hairs are on your head and how many freckles are on your arms. He even knows your favorite color—and your favorite ice-cream flavor. And guess what? He knows your birthday too! Who is he? He is God the Father!

Draw a picture of yourself with your family or add a photograph here.

God the Father knows everything about you because he created you. He made you different from everyone else. You are special—there is no one else like you in the whole world. God the Father knew you before you were born. He loved you then, he loves you now—and he will always love you. What a great Father you have!

When is your birthday?

God created our beautiful world—earth, sea, sky, sun, moon, stars, fish, animals, trees, plants, and flowers. Then he said, "I will make a man and a woman to live here." So he made Adam and Eve. They lived in the Garden of Eden.

Your birthday is the day you were born into God's beautiful world! That was a great day for your mom and dad. God wants you to love his world and take good care of it.

"I knew you before you were born."

JEREMIAH 1:5

Birthdays are a time for singing "Happy Birthday to you!" Who will sing that special song to you this year? It's fun to hear your name being sung. Your mom and dad gave you your name on the day you were born. Your name is important because that's how people know you are you! Maybe you are named after a saint or after one of your grandparents. Ask your mom or dad why they chose your name.

How many letters are in your first name?

8

Who has always known your name—even before your mom and dad called you by your name the very first time? God the Father! Isn't that amazing? That's how much he loves you. The Bible says that God has written your name on the palm of his hand. That means he will never forget you—not even for a moment!

Draw your hand here. Then write your name on it.

Jesus' name is special too! A long time ago, God the Father said to the angel Gabriel, "I have a message for you to deliver." So Gabriel went to visit a young girl in Nazareth called Mary. When Mary saw the angel, she was frightened. But Gabriel said to her, "Don't be afraid. You are going to have a baby, and you are to name him Jesus." Jesus' name means "God saves his people."

"Hail Mary, full of grace,
the Lord is with you."

LUKE 1:28

11

Birthdays are always fun, even if it's not *your* birthday! It's exciting to be invited to a friend's birthday party and to buy and wrap a gift. When you get to the party, there may be balloons and decorations and games to play. There is a birthday cake and ice cream—and lots of other snacks too!

Every year you celebrate the birthday of your special friend, Jesus. Do you know when? December 25—Christmas Day! That's the greatest birthday ever!

12

What would you like to eat at your birthday party?

....

....

....

Jesus loves you and is always with you. That's why he came from heaven to earth—and that's why we have Christmas! One way you can make Jesus happy is by talking to him—anytime and anywhere. Tell him what makes you happy or sad. And remember to tell Jesus every day, "I love you!" That really makes him smile.

What could you say to Jesus right now?

....

....

....

....

Do you know where Jesus was born? In the little town of Bethlehem. Mary laid him in a manger and the animals breathed on him to keep him warm.

Out on the hillsides, an angel appeared to some shepherds and said, "I have good news for you! A Savior has been born."

Suddenly, there were many angels singing, "Glory to God in the highest."

The shepherds said, "Let's go find this baby."
Off they went and found Jesus in the stable.

The shepherds went home praising God.

LUKE 2:20

When you think of birthdays, do you think of gifts? Perhaps you get gifts in your mailbox—and birthday cards too! Isn't it exciting to guess what's inside the bags or boxes!

Gifts are one way to celebrate the day you were born. People who love you have fun deciding what to buy you. Then they enjoy watching the big smile on your face as you open your presents! Remember to say thank you!

Do you know who has given you the most awesome gift? Your Heavenly Father! His gift is Jesus. Jesus came to earth so that we could live with him forever in heaven.

Would you like to give Jesus a gift to thank him for loving you so much? Here are a few ideas. Be kind to your brothers and sisters. Listen to your parents. And say "Sorry" when you've hurt someone. Jesus will love opening those gifts!

What's your favorite birthday gift?

....
....
....
....

What gift can you give Jesus today?

....
....
....
....

When Jesus was a baby, he received three special gifts—gold, frankincense, and myrrh. Who gave Jesus these special presents? Wise men from the East. They had seen a new star in the sky. That meant that a king had been born. So they quickly got on their camels and started their journey. After many months, the star seemed to stop moving.

"This must be the home of the new king," they said.

When Mary saw them, she said, "Come in and visit Jesus."

"The wise men saw the child with Mary, his mother."

MATTHEW 2:11

Moms have birthdays too! Do you celebrate your mom's birthday by giving her a card or a present? A special gift to her would be to say, "Mommy, I love you!" Be sure to hug and kiss her too!

Do you know that we also celebrate the birthday of Jesus' mom? Mary's birthday is on September 8. What a great day to thank Mary for being Jesus' mother! And don't forget to thank St. Joseph. He cared for and protected both Jesus and Mary.

20

When is your mom's birthday?

....

Where is Mary now? She is in heaven with Jesus and all the angels and saints. And did you know that Jesus' mother is your mother too? Mary loves you and is happy to be part of your family. Just like your mom, Mary prays for you. Be sure to ask for her help when you need it!

Draw a picture of Mary in heaven.

Mary helped a bride and groom at their wedding in Cana.
She was there with Jesus and his disciples. During the party,
Mary heard a waiter say, "We have run out of wine."
  She told him, "Do whatever Jesus tells you."
  Jesus said, "Go and fill those jars with water."
  The waiter was surprised when he tasted the water because

Jesus had changed the water into wine! That was Jesus'
first miracle.

Mary said,

"Do whatever he tells you."

JOHN 2:5

Birthdays are a fun time for your parents to remember that special day when you were born. What time of day was it? How much did you weigh? Did you have any hair? Did you have any brothers or sisters then? Ask your mom and dad to get out photos of you when you were just a day or two old!

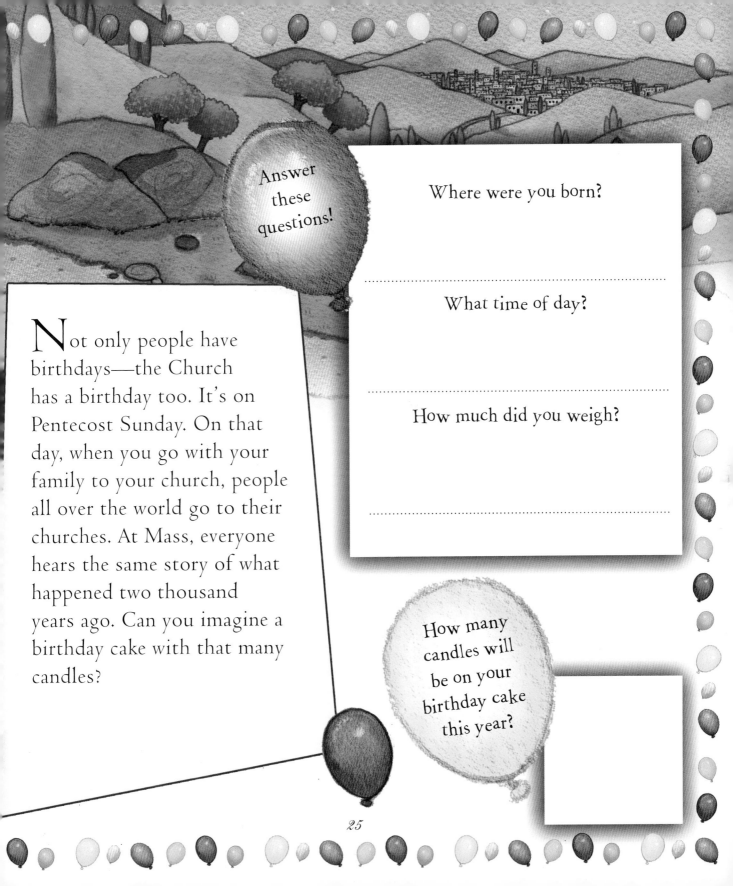

Answer these questions!

Where were you born?

....

What time of day?

....

How much did you weigh?

....

Not only people have birthdays—the Church has a birthday too. It's on Pentecost Sunday. On that day, when you go with your family to your church, people all over the world go to their churches. At Mass, everyone hears the same story of what happened two thousand years ago. Can you imagine a birthday cake with that many candles?

How many candles will be on your birthday cake this year?

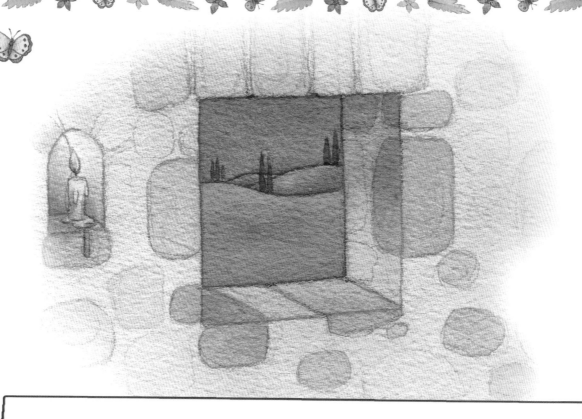

On Pentecost, the disciples and Mary waited in the Upper Room. They prayed and sang songs. Suddenly there was a strong wind. Then flames of fire rested on the disciples' heads.

The disciples said, "The Holy Spirit has come!"

The disciples were excited. They ran outside and told people about Jesus. They were the first Christians. That was how the Church was born.

"They were filled with the Holy Spirit."

ACTS 2:4

My Birthday Prayer

Jesus, I'm so excited that it's my birthday.

I just want to tell you that I'm ☐ years old today!

But you know that, don't you?

Jesus, on my birthday, let me say
thank you for ...
my life,
my mom and dad,
everyone in my family,
my friends,
and especially you!

Jesus, I know you will be with me every day this year.
Keep me healthy, help me with my schoolwork, and
help me to be obedient and kind.

Jesus, I love you. Thank you for being my friend!

Moms and Dads .... This is your page!

From the author:

I have always loved celebrating my birthday. When I was a child, my mother would always prepare a special chicken dish for dinner. My father would give me one tulip for every year of my life, and he would cut out the number of my birthday in the grass.

Memories and traditions are a gift from God—he showers his love on us through our parents. What memories and traditions do you have that you are passing on to your children? Here are some ideas.

Begin your child's birthday with hugs and kisses. Perhaps you could go to Mass, light a candle, pray a decade of the rosary, or read a Bible story.

Intercede: Make sure your child knows you are praying for him in the coming year.

Recall some of the things that God has done in your child's life since her last birthday. Reassure her that he will do lots more in the coming year!

Tell your child what happened on the day he was born.

Honor your child for the good qualities you see in her, such as kindness, helpfulness, or cheerfulness.

Draw attention to what he has achieved during the past year.

Ask your child what she might want to set as a goal for the next year—maybe learning how to read or play a sport.

Yummy foods are such a treat! Let your child decide what she would like to eat for her birthday this year!

Published in 2017 in the U.S. and Canada by
The Word Among Us Press
Frederick, Maryland
www.wau.org

ISBN: 978-1-59325-304-2

Publishing Director: Annette Reynolds
Art Director: Gerald Rogers
Pre-production: Doug Hewitt

Printed and bound in Malaysia
December 2016